Unbelievable Pictures and Facts About Morocco

By: Olivia Greenwood

Introduction

Morocco is a very interesting country. Many people have heard of Morocco because of their well-known Moroccan cuisine. Today we will be learning all about the very exciting country of Morocco.

Will you find any rivers in Morocco?

Morocco is home to many rivers. It is also home to the longest one which is called the Draa river.

What languages do people speak in Morocco?

There are over ten different languages which are spoken in Morocco. However the official language is Arabic, this is what most people speak.

On average how long do people live for in the country?

In Morocco, people usually have quite a long lifespan. They generally live up until 75 years of age on average.

Will you find any deserts in Morocco?

Have you ever heard of the Sahara desert? This is the biggest and hottest desert in the entire world and it is situated in Morocco.

Which sport is their favorite in Morocco?

In Morocco the most popular sport which is played very often and loved by everyone is soccer.

What items do they export the most in the country?

The main items which are exported from the country are textiles, chemicals, and food products.

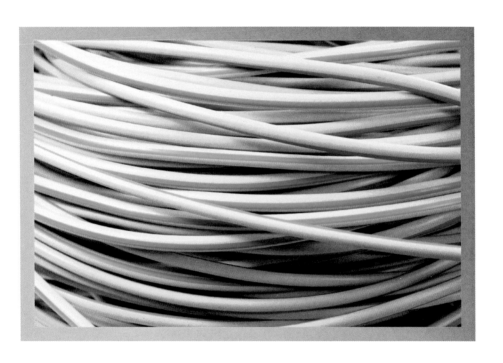

Which religion do they practice the most?

The religion which people have a tendency to follow the most in the country is Islam.

Which city in Morocco is the biggest?

The biggest city in the country of Morocco is Casablanca.

What types of food do people generally eat in Morocco?

People eat all sorts of delicious foods in the country. A common dish includes chicken and couscous.

Where will you find the tallest part of Morocco?

Toubkal is the name of the very highest peak in the country of Morocco.

What money currency do they use in Morocco?

The currency which people use in Morocco is known as the Moroccan dirham.

What is the population size of Morocco?

On average there are currently around 37 million people living in Morocco. How many people live in your country?

Which city is the capital one?

The name of the capital city of Morocco is Rabat.

Were any famous movies filmed in Morocco?

Over the years many popular movies have been filmed in Morocco. Some of the movies include Babel, Kingdom of Heaven, Black Hawk Down, The Mummy Returns and Troy.

Will you find any unique animals in Morocco?

Yes, you will find many unique animals in Morocco. Some of these unique animals include foxes, panthers, jackals, and even gazelles. Do you have any unique animals in your country?

What kind of weather do they have in Morocco?

In Morocco, they have four different unique seasons. When it is winter time it can get really cold. When it is summertime it usually gets very hot and humid.

Does the country have an official name?

Morocco does have an official name. The official name is the Kingdom of Morocco. Does your country have an official name?

Is it safe to travel in Morocco?

Morocco is a really safe place to travel in. The only thing you need to be aware of is small petty crimes like pickpocketing.

Where in the world will you find Morocco?

Morocco has a lot of coastal plains, mountains, and desert lands. The country also has a lot of fertile lands that are used for farming.

What type of landscape does Morocco have?

Morocco has a landscape that is filled with green land, mountains, deserts, and coastal plains.

Made in the USA
Monee, IL
01 November 2019